KT-552-244

This delightful book is the latest in the series of Ladybird books which have been specially planned to help grown-ups with the world about them.

As in the other books in this series, the large clear script, the careful choice of words, the frequent repetition and the thoughtful matching of text with pictures all enable grown-ups to think they have taught themselves to cope. The subject of the book will greatly appeal to grown-ups.

Series 999

THE LADYBIRD
BOOKS FOR GROWN-UPS SERIES

BALLS

by

J.A. HAZELEY, N.S.F.W. and J.P. MORRIS, O.M.G.

(Authors of 'Windmill Warriors: Heroes of Crazy Golf')

Publishers: Ladybird Books Ltd., Loughborough

Printed in England. If wet, Italy.

This is a ball.

A ball can bounce anywhere.

Nobody knows where a ball might go.

But the manager thinks he knows, and the fans think they know and the well–paid pundits think they know, so they speculate about it for most of their waking lives and everybody seems fine with that.

If Ben were only happy when his favourite team did well, he would not be happy very often.

Instead Ben is happy whenever a team he hates does badly.

There are lots and lots of those.

Some sports are more than a game. They have become part of our national identity.

The crack of leather on willow. The gentle clatter of applause as a cherry-red Dukes arcs over the measured sward. Drunken Smurfs messily assembling a forty-foot beer snake.

This is who we are.

"Right, that's it, I'm off," says Carl after the opposing team is awarded a throw-in.

There are still 88 minutes of play left, but Carl knows how these things go.

Mark's wife bought him some tickets to the big match as a treat for working so hard since the twins were born.

Mark met his friends in the pub before—hand.

He cannot remember who won. He cannot remember the score. He cannot remember what game they were playing.

Mark loves sport.

It is the football World Cup.

The famous players from the national team do impossible, beautiful things with the ball in slow-motion in all the advertisements.

Sadly, the team have to play the actual matches at full speed, so they will be going home after the group stage as usual.

A person is considered to be starting an argument about the off–side rule if, when someone asks "what is the off–side rule?" they are nearer to the television than both the person asking "what is the off–side rule?" and the second–last person explaining the off–side rule using empty beer cans and Pringles tubes, unless that person is not actively involved in the argument.

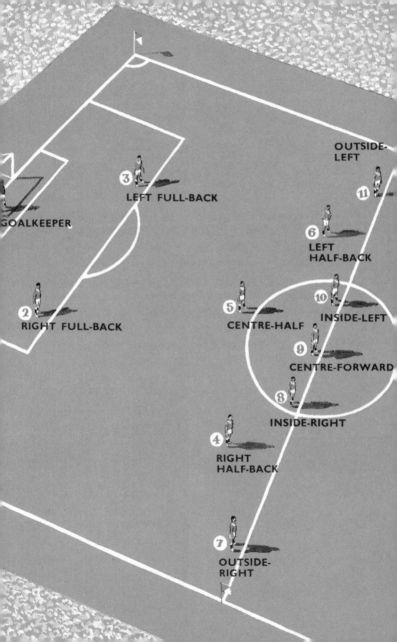

GOALKEEPER

③ LEFT FULL-BACK

② RIGHT FULL-BACK

⑤ CENTRE-HALF

⑥ LEFT HALF-BACK

④ RIGHT HALF-BACK

⑪ OUTSIDE-LEFT

⑩ INSIDE-LEFT

⑨ CENTRE-FORWARD

⑧ INSIDE-RIGHT

⑦ OUTSIDE-RIGHT

Terry is nearing the end of his prison sentence, so has been allowed out on day release. His children are waiting for him on the platform.

"How do you feel about staying with Aunt Pat today, kids?" says Terry.

"Only Barnsworth are playing a friendly at home," he explains. "And I've not seen them in years."

BBC Radio 5 Live has cut away from coverage of the worst mainland terrorist atrocity in decades because there is an important update from the curling.

Otherwise, regular listeners will complain.

Sometimes when we are angry, we want to shout terrible, spiteful things at strangers in the street, but there are laws. We cannot do what we want, even if it makes us feel better.

In a stadium it is different.

You can even set your terrible, spiteful things to music.

Sam has been a county-level fast-bowler since she was ten. She has a season ticket for her local non-league football club and is putting together a Euro Champions League sweepstake in the office.

"You like the men in shorts, eh?" says absolutely everyone to her, all the time. "Those lovely legs!"

Sam could brain them with a cricket ball so quickly they wouldn't know it was her.

Some animals like sport as much as people do.

And when they retire, they can play sport for fun.

These retired race-horses are enjoying a relaxing round of golf.

Every year, Geoff buys his team's replica kit, their replica away kit, a premium TV satellite sports package and a season ticket that costs more than a second–hand car. They usually play so badly that he does not stay for the end.

"Football is the working man's game," says Geoff. "It's not stuck up. It's not like opera."

It is possible to see a world–class opera for around £15.

dad is looking after him
weekend.

ust sit and watch sport
re him," says Kiran's
Kiran's dad. "He's got
k to do."

ne," says Kiran's dad.

It is the quarter finals of the Women's 400kg Welterwidth Berrington, a newly introduced Olympic event in which Team GB have a good chance of a surprise medal placing.

Very few people had heard of the sport before Tuesday, but everybody in the country is suddenly an expert on it now.

Kiran's
for the

"Don't j
and igno
mum to
homewor

"It'll be f

Now he is older, Bob is realistic. He no longer thinks he could, at a push, come on as a maverick substitution from the stands in the 85th minute and put his team level in a vital cup tie.

He is balding and pudgy now and has to stop for breath climbing from the burger stand to his seat.

His fantasies have now moved into management.

For his birthday, Michael always asks for the new Wisden.

He takes the book to his shed at the bottom of the garden and spends his big day looking for mistakes. Then he e-mails Wisden with corrections.

Happy birthday, Michael.

The umpire or referee must know all the laws of the game.

Otherwise players may try and take advantage to help themselves or distract their opponents.

This team has found loopholes in the umpire's knowledge of recent rulings on both bat size and Slade impressions.

Vince has been a fan of Framley North End since he was six. He watches them play every week, through flashes of triumph and troughs of defeat. He is a loyal supporter, and will be until the day he dies and is buried in a Framley North End coffin.

Vince cannot imagine what his life would have been like if he had supported another team.

Probably identical, apart from the colour of the coffin.

Now he is older, Bob is realistic. He no longer thinks he could, at a push, come on as a maverick substitution from the stands in the 85th minute and put his team level in a vital cup tie.

He is balding and pudgy now and has to stop for breath climbing from the burger stand to his seat.

His fantasies have now moved into management.

For his birthday, Michael always asks for the new Wisden.

He takes the book to his shed at the bottom of the garden and spends his big day looking for mistakes. Then he e-mails Wisden with corrections.

Happy birthday, Michael.

The umpire or referee must know all the laws of the game.

Otherwise players may try and take advantage to help themselves or distract their opponents.

This team has found loopholes in the umpire's knowledge of recent rulings on both bat size and Slade impressions.

Vince has been a fan of Framley North End since he was six. He watches them play every week, through flashes of triumph and troughs of defeat. He is a loyal supporter, and will be until the day he dies and is buried in a Framley North End coffin.

Vince cannot imagine what his life would have been like if he had supported another team.

Probably identical, apart from the colour of the coffin.

Brocklyn Fudginelli of the San Domingo Thunderjacks is one of the most famous athletes in the United States of America.

In other countries, sports stars can earn even more by taking up lucrative offers to play in overseas leagues.

Unfortunately for Mr Fudginelli, no—one else on the planet cares about whatever this sport might be that he is doing here.

During the First World War, soldiers stopped fighting to play football in No–Man's–Land.

Hostilities then resumed until the Allies defeated Germany in 1918.

Historians agree that had it not ended so decisively, Germany would almost certainly have won the war on penalties.

"We have walked many miles," pants Darabont.

"Do you have Sky Sports?"

THE AUTHORS would like to record their gratitude and offer their apologies to the many Ladybird artists whose luminous work formed the glorious wallpaper of countless childhoods. Revisiting it for this book as grown-ups has been a privilege.

MICHAEL JOSEPH

UK | USA | Canada | Ireland | Australia
India | New Zealand | South Africa

Michael Joseph is part of the Penguin Random House group of companies whose addresses can be found at global.penguinrandomhouse.com

First published 2017
002

Printed in Italy by L.E.G.O. S.p.A

A CIP catalogue record for this book is available from the British Library

ISBN: 978–0–718–18871-9

www.greenpenguin.co.uk

Penguin Random House is committed to a sustainable future for our business, our readers and our planet. This book is made from Forest Stewardship Council® certified paper.

Many players perform special celebrations when they do well.

This fly-half may have forgotten his kit and been made to do the Six Nations in his vest and pants, but he still celebrates a try by jumping right over the posts.

Ali's team hate their local rivals. It is something to do with a refereeing decision in **1938**.

When the plumber comes round to fix her sink, Ali swaps her team badge tooth—mug for an unmarked glass in case the plumber is a rival fan.

She does not want him sticking her toothbrush anywhere unsavoury.